Table of contents

<u>Rule 25: Happiness and its pursuit</u>

<u>Table of summaries</u>

Rules of the rules

(A quick byword)

Each of the rules is important but it's up to the reader to decide on which take paramount. I struggled quite a bit on the order as some of them may seem to contradict each other but it's up to you the reader to decide on which rules are more important than others to you.

I won't pander to you, I'm not here to hold your hand and guide you through this, because you're an adult or chances are have the intellect of one, too many people treat others like they are speaking to idiots so I will give you the benefit of the doubt.

This is a work of opinion if you agree with my sentiments great if not well to each their own, you are your own individual, how and what you think are probably not going to be a carbon copy of my own thought process.

Each rule will be summed up with a catchy epilogue term that sort of sums up what the rules is really about if both possible and appropriate.

(WARNING) contains bad language where appropriate.

Rule 1: Forgiveness

I am not a religious man, so before you get the wrong idea, this is nothing to do with religion, none of that "turn the other cheek" or "love thy neighbour", nothing wrong with that, but that's not what I am talking about. I'm talking about forgiveness, mostly the forgiveness of self, many of us have done things, said things in our past that we are not proud of, whether through action or inaction.

That regret is an anchor dragging you down. Worse, we justify our actions when in our heart we know we are in the wrong. It is something holding us down and many of us never deal with it, regardless of if it was fear, indecision, anger or embarrassment, in a lot of cases it is ourselves who punish us the most for our past actions.

Now, not everything can be forgiven and I'm not absolving anyone's actions, there is real evil in this world and sometimes things are done that cannot be forgiven, but for the majority of people the things we have done are not that bad, yet we agonise over our actions,

Seriously wise up, I am not saying it'll happen overnight but learn to forgive yourself. I don't know you, I don't know if you deserve to be forgiven, but you know who does?

You!

And on the point of forgiving others, yea people can be pretty terrible, they can hurt you, ruin you and not even care or worse yet relish in the experience, we see it all around us, when you were in school there were those who bullied others, and those who were bullied when you were older, you saw people who were head over heels in love one day, then hated each other with a passion the next.

Yea some people are terrible, but if you were ever on the receiving end of someone's hate, don't let it consume you, hell don't let it affect you, I'm not saying don't stand up for yourself, personally I've punched a few people who deserved it. Was it the right thing to do? Yes, yes it was.

And anyone who was ever harassed back in school or in the workplace does remember it.

As you can probably tell I was bullied back in school, but that is just me, and yea for a long time it was something I carried with me. But in at the end of the day, why should I care? Why should you?

Maybe forgiveness isn't the right term for what I'm getting at but it's pretty close, I guess letting go would be more accurate. Not everything can be forgiven but, given time, everything can be atoned for.

Rule 1 Summary

<u>Life is too short for the baggage.</u>

Rule 2: Choice and consequence

You have a choice, there is no such thing as a situation where you didn't have a choice, regardless of your past actions or anything that leads you into a situation always remember from this point on you havea choice in your life and every one of your decisions has consequences. But if you follow your heart (I know sappy, but true) then at least at the end of the day you'll have no regrets, or at least if things go wrong you tried your hardest.

So many people think they are helpless in the grand scheme of things, like people who think only two or three parties have a hope in most elections, so they vote for one guy because they like him more than the other guy? Imagine if you voted for the guy (or girl) you actually wanted to win?

""oh but you'd be throwing away your vote"" maybe, but better than throwing away your right to make a real choice, besides wouldn't it be beautiful if everyone did that?

Of course lest we forget, although we have choice there is always a consequence. Yes you can do basically anything you want in this world. But should you? No, god no! Listen if you want to walk naked down the street you can, that's your choice, but you will be arrested. My point is every action no matter how small or insignificant has consequences, maybe small and insignificant but consequences all the same. Say you have an extra sugar in your coffee?

Well on the tiniest level your decision means yes your coffee may taste better, but you also contribute to tooth decay. Tiny as consequences go, still valid though. Now I'm not saying to let actions and their aftermath consume you, chances are thousands of your decisions every day have such tiny consequences or even bigger ones that don't affect you, and many of the ones that do affect you positively, but what I am getting at is the bigger choices the big decisions, if you don't think about how they will affect you, chances are they will, maybe badly?

Always remember that a large amount of your choices don't just affect you either, they affect the people around you, mostly your friends and family but not just them, you choices can and will change who you are as a person, and that can have a ripple effect, in fact it probably will, and that's only talking about personal choices, there are all kinds of choices.

So if you can, think about how your decisions don't just affect you, but affect the world around you.

Rule 2 Summary

<u>Think before you act.</u>

Rule 3: Opinion

Oh you have an opinion? Congratulations you are a human being, is your opinion valid? Well of course you are a person, besides an outsiders opinion can pick up on some part of the situation others may have overlooked, is your opinion as valid as say someone who knows what they are talking about? No sit down, shut up and listen,

People will always develop an opinion many times instantly, even you, right now have opinions about this book, am I a visionary? Slightly amusing? Or to you is this merely the ravings of a mad man, maybe it's boring as sin, in which case kudos for sticking it out this long thanks for the benefit of the doubt, maybe you feel you have some insight into my thought process or who I am as a person, now is your opinion on me valid? Yes, is it as valid as say my friend of ten years? My brother?Even one of my enemy's?No, sit down, shut up and listen.

There is a right and a wrong time to express your right to free speech and your opinion, and if you feel strongly about something? Great fight the bit out. (Within reason).There is a particular group in Britain, who I won't even do the decency of referring to by name, who take this far past any reasonable level, who spew hatred and sectarianism, for no reason except ignorance and arrogance of anyone not born in Britain, and of anyone who is but is of a different religion. And although their arrogance is disgusting, it's their ignorance that is truly astounding. Basically they are like a cult, because the people at the top lie incessantly and the people further down lap it up.

This is a time of free information, when you have all the knowledge of history at your fingertips, only a mouse click away. For fucks sake research something before you talk about it and take anything you hear with a pinch of salt.

So I leave you this chapter dear reader with a quote by Evelyn Beatrice Hall

(I know, how pretentious of me)

-I disapprove of what you say, but I will defend to the death your right to say
it-

Rule 3 Summary

<u>We don't all get to have an opinion.</u>

Rule 4: The importance of words

I'm quite a long winded individual (if you hadn't picked that up from the book of basically my rants you've been reading)

But even I wish that wasn't so, yes I wouldn't be me if I wasn't, but I have always envied those that speak only when they have something important to say, cause I always find myself listening the most to them, and always find I think on those words later. I've met a lot of people in my short life and some were brilliant, a lot were idiots, but I would classify myself as an idiot, I speak my mind too much, and don't expect people to listen too much, cause if I met me? I wouldn't listen to half of what I have to say.

I'm the sort to put my foot in my mouth, then over think and over explain why, it's a terrible trait that has cost me people who were very important to me, maybe this rule is a little biased for me, and maybe it only applies to one in a hundred of you, but it's still something that should be said and it's something I'm trying to do with this whole book, maybe to remind myself, and to remind one out of one hundred of you, that for our words to carry impact, they've got to be our words, they say you should think with your head and feel with your heart, but I say, why not use both? (I know sappy as hell) but I am a product of people, who I've met, who I've known, and who I am, as are we all. Hmm food for thought I guess.

I'm not saying every time words escape your lips they have to be works of brilliance or some before unheard of ideal or understanding, we are people, and people talk, we talk of small things, some important to us, most not. But I just wish that when the time comes to say something worthwhile, it's worthwhile.

So what I'm getting at is not to let the important things go unsaid, and maybe leave off some of the other stuff, that's what I'm going to try to do at least.

Rule 4 Summary

You can't unsay things so say what sticks.

Rule 5: Sorry

A lot of us know when we have done something wrong, said something wrong, hurt another whether on purpose or accidently, through word or action, and we apologise, maybe we don't. Maybe something stops us, anger or pride or shame, but sometimes something stops us, maybe sometimes we don't realise we hurt them, or we feel it was deserved. But anger fades, pride is bitter but we swallow it anyway and shame? If you feel ashamed of what you have done then apologising is the first step to making up for what you did. Sometimes apologising isn't easy, sometimes you lose your chance to, or it's taken from you, so don't let that happen, make amends while you can. Because even with the greatest anger it will keep you warm, but it will burn you up inside, with the greatest pride it won't keep you warm at night, it won't make you happy, and shame will poison you inside.

I'm not saying you always need to apologise, personally I've never had a problem with it, if I'm in the wrong, but if not there is no force on earth will make me apologise when I've done no wrong and I know that may sound selfish or prideful, but it leads me on to my next point about this.

It may seem like a serious paradox of what I just said but stop apologising, I know it's a funny thing, I just said how itsimportant to while you have the chance but on the other side of the coin there are those who say sorry to much, who have done no wrong but always seem to end up apologising, if you're in the wrong you should know it, and you better damn well know it when you're not.

There was a Harvard study in the past that said people who apologise a lot are a lot more likeable. And maybe this is just personal opinion but that sounds like crap to me, I've met people who apologised incessantly and it was annoying as hell, again this is my opinion and maybe I only feel this way because it goes against my views on the matter.

But seriously if you have done no wrong you have no business apologising, because pride may be bitter but it's still yours, and it is your right to keep it,

I get the feeling this pages summary may be obvious but none too catchy

Rule 5 Summary

<u>Sorry when sorry is due.</u>

Rule 6: Acceptance & death

This book may be many things, but its heart it's about happiness, about how to find happiness in your life and the many reasons both simple and complex that stop us from finding it, this chapter is probably the simplest to understand, but the hardest to really convey in words, but here goes.

Acceptance is the 5th stage of grief, and from both a morbid and uplifting way this too applies to life, life in its own way is an acceptance of death, which sadly many of us don't or can't accept, for anyone who doesn't know the stages of grief they are denial, anger, bargaining, depression and acceptance, and these are all pivotal emotions we go through in our lives, who at one point doesn't think, that death will never catch them, that they would live forever? And both anger and bargaining tie in together in many religions, the prospect of religion is that if you do this, then you get to live forever, in heaven, and we have all seen people driven to great anger over religion, hatred even,
depression is a little harder to explain, I mean the thought that one day you will be gone, yea that depressing, we are all of ourselves, and no one knows us like we know ourselves, so the thought that one day we will be gone, and no one will really, really know who we were, not like we know ourselves, is damn depressing, but as I said this chapter is about acceptance, and again, it is awful to try and convey what I'm getting at, but you need to accept yourself.

One day we will all be gone, but not today, today we are truly, gloriously alive, and every day we have, every day we rip from the jaws of oblivion is another day we are alive, another day we beat the odds, so don't just accept that your alive, don't just accept who you are, celebrate it.

One day you will be gone, and no one for the rest of history could possibly replace you, because you are you, and there will never be another so take pride in that fact, and accept your place as a wholly unique piece of the universe.

Of course another part of acceptance in life is you know, that at some point life will shiton you from a great height, it's going to happen, probably way more than once, but we all need to learn to accept what we can't change, and accept our responsibility with what we can change,

Rule 6 Summary

<u>When life gives you lemons.</u>

Rule 7: Love

Love, love is the simplest thing to explain in this world, and because of that there's nothing I need to tell you, there's nothing I need to say about love, and yet this chapter is for me, because love is something that is entirely up to the individual, love is something inherent to humankind, love is a personal thing, who and how you love is yours entirely, and no love is wrong, no one is wrong about love, except the people that argue that love is just a chemical reaction, screw those guys, bunch of miserable bastards.

no love isn't just chemicals in your brain, love isn't just who we want to mate with or who we really like, love is love, and its literally the greatest, most amazing, most beautiful thing about life, love can move mountains, love can traverse the globe, and love is something that truly can never be described. loveis wholly unique. What you think of as love and what I think of as love may be so much more different than you can imagine, but it's still love, because it's unique to the individual, and every individual is unique.

No one gets to decide who you love, least of all you, one day you just realise that it's her, or him, or who ever, and that they are enough, because they are far more than you ever realised you needed.

Love is unexplainable and indescribable to me really, but I will give it a shot here, and probably not convey a single thing I mean.

I believe in love, maybe not true love, or any of that predestined crap. but I believe in love, I know love, for me, love is that person that when you talk to them, everything else falls away, and in those lucky moments you are just you, and they are just them, and that's enough.

Rule 7 Summary

<u>Love is love need I say more?</u>

Rule 8: Excess

The problem with the pursuit of happiness is that there are so many things that can bring a sense of joy or fulfilment, and although many of them are actually positive building blocks toward happiness many are not, I'm speaking of the physical things that can instil a sense or state of being within us, such as drugs, alcohol, sex, cigarettes to name a few.

now I'm not going to tell you how to live your life, your an adult you can make your own choices, and I'm not going to be so two dimensional as to say any of these things are bad, but it's up to the individual not the thing to decide if these things are bad or good, but I will say this, everything in moderation, that's the deference between the recreational drug user and the habitual, it's the difference between an adult and a sex addict, the difference between an evening out, and crippling alcoholism, you get the point.

of course these are only a few examples, I mean come on popping bubble wrap can become addictive, if you have enough free time, and a large enough supply of bubble wrap.
we all have our vices, and there is nothing wrong with that, but if you feel something is becoming a problem, or if the people around you, the people you care about, or value the opinion of, think something's becoming a problem, then it's time to take a good hard look at yourself, and your actions, also a good rule of thumb is, if your ashamed of it, and can't stop, its addiction.

Excess is just having way too much of something, and even then not all excess is bad, who doesn't want too much money? whodoesn't want an excess of personality, who could put a price on having way too much time? But although excess can't be clear cut as a good or bad thing, the dark truth of it is that it's usually excess that poisons us in the end.

I like to end my chapters with a snappy little line, which can be argued, is an excess of writing, or an excess of opinion I guess, funny it is then, that just this once I can't give you one little line that encapsulates what I mean.
Funnier still I can give you two, I know how excessive of me?

Rule 8 Summary

<u>If some is good, more must be better.</u>

<u>Sometimes just enough, is all you need.</u>

Rule 9: Patience

They say good things come to those who wait, and maybe so, of course it's entirely subjective because if you take too long, the thing you want can slip through your fingers. But it's not all or nothing. And having a little patience doesn't hurt after all. So bide your time.

Of course on the other hand it's far too easy to do nothing, to think or hope that things will work themselves out, which isn't really how any of this works is it? Sometimes you got to take the leap, and sometimes it's better to let someone else leap first and see what happens, but that depends on you, and it depends on the situation, so I can't really tell you which one is right, but I can tell you that, if it turns out you should have leapt and you regret not taking that chance, then it's a lot harder to get back to that place a second time, sometimes impossible, and should you be faced again with that dilemma.

Then I wish you luck on your decision.

They say patience is the best virtue, I never got that, I'd say it was kindness, I think patience is just something that is hard to understand, it's hard to know when patience becomes inaction.

I think patience is an important point and it really is a rule of life; but I can't really tell you to endorse something that I don't have that firm a grasp on myself. Personally patience has never been my strong suit, I'm more the rush in and either fuckup massively or somehow come across as charming, but that a real 90%/10% split.

I'm kind of a renowned idiot on this point and I wish I wasn't, but I plan to work on that, and that's the point of this book isn't it? To highlight the things most of us know, but a lot of us have probably forgotten.

So I'm going to work on that, and maybe you should too?

Couldn't hurt after all, could it?

Really all you can say about patience, and about its place in your life, is to be decisive, make the decision you are going to make, even if it is to wait, still make that decision and stand by it.

Rule 9 Summary

<u>Early birds, worms and such.</u>

Rule 10: Change

We are all changing throughout our lives, every decision we make, every situation we are in, and every moment we think, you're not the same person you were five years ago, you're not even the same person you were 5 minutes ago, regardless of if any of my writing has sunk in.

You're always told to be yourself in life, that is not really true but you can't tell someone to be someone else though, because that is quite shallow. I'll let you in on the trick of it though, just be who you want to be, this is your life, you decisions are your own, not anyone else.

So be yourself, be someone else, or my personal recommendation be whoever the hell you want to be in this life. if you only get one go round, so neither you, me or anyone else wants to get to the end of it all, look back and be like "damn I hated that guy/girl" that is just not worth it.

Becoming who you want to be isn't always easy, frankly it'll be hard as hell sometimes, but we are all constantly changing so you might as well aim toward being that sort of person. real change isn't easy, and I'm not going to sugar-coat it for you, because if you want to change who you are, you have to put in so much effort, but if you can become the person you want to be, isn't it all worth it?

I'm not saying that you have to change, or that you even want to, just that it's possible, that you have that capability inside yourself, and that you should remember that, in case you ever need it.

If you wake up one day, and you realise you're not the sort of person you wished you were, then you're the only one who going to change that situation.

Making changes in your life is the easiest part of changing who you are, little changes lead to big results after all, but always remember, change for you, never change for someone else, you will run into people in this life who want to change you for themselves, we all run into them, and even with the best intentions, they have no right to try to change you, that's your privilege alone. So if you must change for someone else, let it be your decision, and let who you become be your decision alone, change for someone else, for yourself.

Rule 10 Summary

<u>Change is changing.</u>

Rule 11: Anxiety

It's perfectly normal to be anxious about things, you can't know everything after all, and the outcome of events can't be predicted one hundred percent, every action has a reaction and all that, but when it comes right down to it, anxiety is the thing that will lead to the most regrets in life, it can lead to all the things you should have done, all the things you wanted to do, that you didn't, and when you look back on it, you can ask yourself why? But there is no good real answer.

Anxiety is this fake wall you put up in your head; it can be a thousand and one reasons not to do something, but when you realise that that is all it is, a fake wall made of fake reasons, and the only real reason not to do something, not to make a decision is that you are scared, and it's ok to be scared, we all get scared at some point but fear is the mortar that holds that fake wall together.

Fear is a reaction, but inaction is a choice, and once you make the choice to act, then that wall has nothing holding it together, and it will come crashing down.

Now this chapter isn't just for people who feel they suffer from anxiety, it's for everyone because on at least some low level it affects everyone, anyone can be put in a situation that makes them anxious, and for anyone who it might be a daily occurrence, it's important that the awareness is out there. It's not something that you can force someone to overcome, and it's not as easy as simply telling them to get over it, that transformation has to come from them, or yourself in case this affects you on a personal level.

If you know someone who is affected by anxiety on a serious level, the only advice that can be given is to support them if they make any effort to be more outgoing, or overcome whatever is causing their anxiety, but don't try to force them, don't force them into any situation where you expect them to sink or swim, because even with the best intentions that is a sure fire way to send them spiralling.

I have met many people in my life who acknowledge this part of themselves, and some who would classify themselves as suffering from it, in the past or now, and they understand it better, at least their personal brand of it, than you or I or anyone else will.

Even I have been put in situations, sometimes even situations I sought, and when it came to the moment, I froze, and "I can't do this" or "I don't want to do this" was all that was in my head, and on occasion I rose above, other times I didn't, and it can be a stupidly simple as jumping into a river to go swimming with your friends, which sadly I didn't put my whole heart into, funny thing is, even for something as pointless as that memory, I wish I had done it, and that memory is a very powerful tool for me, because now when I'm in those sorts of situations, I remember that, and I take that leap.

Rule 11 Summary

<u>Push down the wall.</u>

Rule 12: Depression

By now you probably have a good understanding of what I would say here, something along the lines of "the power is in you to pull yourself out of anything, because no one else is going to do it for you" and yea, that's my usual wheel house, but on this subject no, no that's not the way to go about this.

Truth be told this is something that hits me hard, there was a time in my life that I could see no way forward, I was in so much pain, and the people who I would have turned to for help, were the ones who caused it.

That was my darkness and people I cared for, people I would have killed for, would have died for, chose to push me into it, and honestly that is something that I'm always going to carry with me, it's a part of me now, and it wasn't a part of myself I chose, other people took that right from me.

So as far as advice goes for depression, it is what it is and there is no easy answer, I wouldn't do anyone the disservice of saying there is.

No one else saved me from depression, and I didn't save myself, it may seem cliché, but time healed me, because time heals all wounds as they say. Gradually that part of my life was put behind me, and one day I woke up, and it was manageable, and every day since, it's easier.

The things that have happened to me, the things that pushed me to my furthest, and I'm not being dramatic, there have been things that almost broke me, almost took me to a place I know I wouldn't have come back from.

Those things are kind of like a deep cut, it heals, it hurts like hell but it heals, and then one day it's a scab, and you know it's going to hurt but you still pick at it, but it hurts a little less than you remember doesn't it? But one day even the scabs gone and it's just a scar.

That's the thing you carry with you the longest isn't it, the scar? But maybe if we are lucky, and enough time passes, even that will fade?

If this is something that affects you, or someone close to you, I can't tell you how to fix it, I can only relate my experiences, and I hope that helps in some small way. We all have our battle scars, we all have those things that have happened to us, the people we lost, and the dark times we have gone through, it's not something easily fixed, but it's something we have to acknowledge.

Rule 12 summary

<u>Give it time.</u>

Rule 13: Importance of fun

Life is short, and if you take it too seriously it will be both short and boring, and no one wants that,
take your interests, take your hobbies, take all the things you find fun, and revel in them.

I'm often described as dorky or weird because of my interests, and I am fine with that, I am a full grown man, who has had serious discussions with people about things ranging from Disney movies, all the way to advanced particle physics, I have cracked Pokémon jokes to other full grown men and had them in stitches, and I have done many stupid crazy things in my life, why?

For the fun of it, so embrace the things you like that are stupid or weird to other people, don't ever feel that your interests have to coincide with others. One of the points I have kind of been flogging a dead horse over in this book, is individuality, you are you, I am me, he/she/it are he/she/ it catch my drift? My point is, have fun, do the things you find fun, have the ideas that amuse and interest you, never let anyone shut down what makes you you.

Because it happens, it's awful but it does, you might meet someone who is brilliant and vibrant and beautiful, and that is great, but unfortunately there are other people in this world, who choose to undermine people like that, who choose to ridicule or attack, and generally choose to make someone else's life a little bit worse, because they don't understand, or they don't care, or just maybe they want to make themselves feel a little bit better about themselves.

Never be ashamed of the things that make you weird and wonderful, because they make you both weird and exceedingly wonderful, and that is awesome. We are living in the most accepting time in human history; sure we still got problems and shit, issues of race, sexuality, religion, gender, human rights, but we are getting there. That got a little serious for a point about fun didn't it? Well digression is my strong suit, but let's getback on topic.

You know what one of my main interests is? Videogames, I love it, I love every facet of it, from the industry, the game mechanics, the storylines, the music, even the way videogame journalism is changing right now, and I love it all. This is a perfectly valid interest, and not because of any of a million reasons I could give you, its valid because of just one.

It's my interest, I find it fun, and I enjoy it, and that is enough of reason. So what interests you?

Rule 13 summary

<u>Life is short; don't let it be short and boring.</u>

Rule 14: Action & Duality of human nature

Don't misunderstand, I'm not about to take on some lofty ideal and persona, I would be full of shit and you would see that, in fact some of you reading probably think I've been full of shit from the beginning, and maybe so, but what I am talking about now, about our duality I've only really come to understand while writing this, and not because of the writing style, or because of the subject matter, but because I'm writing this.

All the things I put in, everything I leave out, whether I ramble or not and what I am trying to convey to you dear reader. It's a matter of duality, what I say and what I mean. Even in everyday life that existsid say, it's in what we do, what we think we should do, and of course what we want to do as well, the third option as it were? But these are all a matter of choice and not about action, and maybe it's our choices that define who we are to ourselves, but it's most certainly our actions that define us to the world.

Maybe I'm too jaded for my age, and my outlook reflects that sometimes, but when I look at people I know, when I see the personas they develop, nurture and portray, and how different they are from the people who inhabit them, I guess it saddens me. And maybe I'm just being simple or naive, but I can't understand how they can expect to be find happiness if they refuse to let the world see them for who they really are. And of course I know I'm probably as guilty of this as anyone. But I am glad and I am happy that there are a few people I love, who I know, know me. And accept me for who I am. But the only reason I have that, is because I let them know me, and know who I am.

I have friends who struggle with issues, who have chosen to impart in me their biggest secrets, they're greatest issues, and facts about themselves that they thought they could never share with another, and maybe I'm uniquely suited in their eyes to know these things, to ponder them, and give my honest opinion and support to them, if anything I am proud that they feel that way toward me.

But in another way it's a little sad, that they don't feel they can live openly endorsing these parts of themselves, out of shame or fear of recrimination, and it's not my place to speak for them but I always advise them, to let their actions speak for them, and to accept who they are, because hiding from the fact, or hiding from the part of yourself, doesn't change anything, because you only end up hurting yourself, and worse you hurt those who truly do worry for you.

As often I digress though, my main point about duality and its presence in human nature is pretty simple though, there's always that little nagging voice in the back of your head that tells you what you want to do, who you want to be, and what you want to be doing, but all too often we ignore that voice, and in fact our actions are the opposite of it, we feel we have to be or act a certain way which isn't true, at least it shouldn't be.

Rule 14 summary

<u>You are more than one thing, so why pretend you're not?</u>

Rule 15: Anger

Things like rage and anger are a big part of life, anger against perceived injustices against us, and rage against injustices in general, there are a thousand and one reasons to be angry, and ridiculously we are taught now days to express our anger, while simultaneously just going about our days, and I use the word "ridiculously" very validly in this situation.

when you teach people to express every little bit of anger, then people will associate anger with the adrenaline it gives them, now I'm not saying to repress your anger either, that way you just end up getting walked all over your entire life, until you snap, and punch someone in the face.

Now every now and then someone disserves a good punch in the face, but that is beside the point, what I'm really trying to convey here is balance, anger is ok, where it's appropriate, but don't let it consume you, and obviously make sure to let some things go.

It's ok to get angry about things, when there's a legit reason to be angry, on the other hand though anger can literally kill you, and you don't want to go through your life filled with anger anyway. You might see a thousand things in one day that piss you off, and you let it slide, but then there is one thing that throws your switch, and you let hell loose.

There is no real definitive thing you can say about anger, it's not an all or nothing thing, and it's not something I can recommend or dissuade any of you from, some of us need a little more anger in our lives, and some of us a little less really. In the case of anger as a part of this life, I think what needs to be said is that it is a part of us, all of us, and acknowledging that it is there may sometimes be enough, I don't regard myself as an angry person, but I know there are things that make me absolutely livid, it's the same with most of us, and really, just being aware that you have that inside you is a crucial piece of understanding the puzzle that makes up you.

There is no right answer to "when you should get angry" because that's not something I can know about you, that not something anyone can know about you, except you.

Rule 15 Summary

<u>Angers the dog in all of us, but it's our choice if it barks, or it bites.</u>

Rule 16: Courage

"Courage is not the absence of fear, but rather the judgement that something else is more important than one's fear". That's a quote by Ambrose Redmoon and although I hate to be that guy who quotes anything other than movies. I felt that it was a great point and that it really encapsulates the most important thing about courage, and if you want my opinion, which by this point let's face it, you do, otherwise why are you still reading this? But in my opinion there are three real types of courage.

The courage to put yourself at risk for something important, like the fire-fighters who rush into burning buildings, nothing but respect for those people, The courage to accept the worst and to stand strong against it, there are people in this world who are just dealt a bad hand at times, like those who are diagnosed with terrible illnesses and such, something I may never understand, but am incredibly humbled by.

The third type, is the one we are probably all most familiar with, the courage to stand for something, or to not let something else stand, and this can be as small hearing a racist, homophobic, or sectarian comment and calling the speaker out on it, or just saying no to a situation you do not want to be a part of, now this may seem like a small courage, and nothing compared to the first two, I'm not going to tell you "no its just as important" because yea its usually not, but it's still important none the less, a small flame can light a huge darkness after all.

courage isn't just in how we deal with others though, obviously courage is a personal thing, in how we face any situation, most decisions and generally in our everyday life, so the best advice I can give on that, is if in any situation, you think something is the "courageous thing to do" that generally means it's what you want to do, and maybe it's something your too scared to do, but in future, just every now and then, if something feel like it's the courageous thing to do, then choose that option take that leap, because that's what you truly want to do, and don't let anything hold you back, let alone yourself.

if we all just had a little more courage, if we took all those lessons we learned as kids to heart, if even just a little more often, we didn't take the safe choice, the easy choice, and instead spoke up, if we stood for something, this world would be a hell of a lot better, For you, for me and for everyone else. So I will leave off this chapter dear reader with a request, hell I would even go so far as to say I am begging you. If you see something that wrong, something that shouldn't be tolerated or if you see something that is hurting another, then stand up, be heard and stop that shit in its tracks.

Rule 16 Summary

<u>One spark can light the fuse, because sometimes one spark is all it takes.</u>

Rule 17: Honesty

Honesty is important because, well let's face I don't really need to explain that do I? Of course there is more than one kind of honesty, and I won't preach total 100% honesty all the time, I mean come on here, to borrow an incredibly well worn stereotype if your significant other asks "does my butt look big in this?" there is not one on this earth brave or stupid enough to answer honestly in that situation. But as always I digress, another form of honesty which is all too tragically often overlooked is admittance. This is arguably the most important type of honesty, admitting things to ourselvesand to others.

They say the first step to overcoming addiction is admitting you have a problem after all. That might not be the lightest of subjects for a rule on honesty so let me point out a more positive aspect, there can be a great strength to be found in honestly admitting things, in sharing our hopes and dreams with others, our fears and weaknesses too, because there is nothing stronger than a supportive person in your life, even if that support comes only from yourself. I know I would have never published this book without the support and on occasion nagging influence of certain people.

In the spirit of admittance, I've got to confess something even now, I had no clue how you would define this book, and I wrote the damn thing, is it self-help? Doubtful, I'm not really judging anyone or telling them how to improve themselves, and even if I did, who am I to judge you? I don't know you, I know nothing about you. I'm basically just telling you my opinion on life, and a few of the millions of things that make up us? If anything I hope I'm being helpful in some small way to you the reader, and maybe reminding you of a few small things that may have slipped your mind in the grand scheme of things.

But mostly I'm ranting and going off on tangents like this. If anything it's a book of philosophy, with sprinklings of crap humour and far too much of one man from time to time.

Another point I should make on honesty is that you should never trust a dishonest person, so you should never be a dishonest person, if it's your actions that define you, then it's your words that tell your story.

Now if you see any paradoxes in my writing or if at times I seem to contradict myself, well that is bound to happen, humans are walking paradoxes after all, and I'm not so dumb or so arrogant to thing you're so dumb, that you're not going to notice that, from time to time as it happens. All a part of the honesty people.

Rule 17 Summary

<u>You know not to trust dishonest people, so why be dishonest?</u>

Rule 18: Connections

Connecting is a huge part of this life, because we were never meant to have to stand alone, and try as we might we will always be part of something bigger, be it your family, your friends and your colleagues, alas we don't get to pick our family or our colleagues for the most part, and when it comes to our friends? Well they are basically family aren't they, If they really are our friends?

Because family isn't just your blood, it is who you would bleed for. every connection you make in life is important, major and minor, even if you don't realise it, because the people you love, and the people you hate, even the random people you run into in some small way changed who you are, they made you better, or worse or just stranger, and it's all been worth it, even the bits that feel like they haven't.

Friendship specifically is one of the biggest factors in who we are and who we become, because even from a young age they are the first people we choose to let influence us, in hopefully positive ways, and you don't need all the friends in the world, you just need the ones who make your world bigger.

This is the part where I usually go off on a little personal tangent, you know give a little insight into why I think the way I do, and my hope is that by doing so you will relate more to me, and relate more to what I'm saying, hopefully you will take some of all this to heart?

But in the case of friendship, I have friends who are nothing like me, never were, never will be, a lot of us met when we were teenagers, and we did a lot of stupid things, had some great adventures, occasionally put ourselves in danger, my jaw still aches at a particular memory involving a large amount of alcohol, a stolen ladder and some bad advice. But that's a little too personal to share.

Still I love them like they are my own brothers and sisters and they have taught me some great, stupid and frankly brilliant things, like how to open a tin can with a knife, how to make balloon animals, and that life is far too short to care about matching socks. Oh, and also how not to slide down a ladder like a fireman.

Connecting with people is important, not always easy, but always important, and it's sad when we end up not being able to connect to the people we wish we had, or worse if we realise we squandered a connection to someone else, and we never realised how important we were to them. None of us are going to be here forever, so what is stopping us from being there for them right now?

Rule 18 Summary

<u>Who would you bleed for?</u>

<u>Life is far too short for matching socks.</u>

Rule 19: Legacy

If everything I have wrote so far, has been some form of balance, a weighing up of the pros and cons of many facets of life, then the subject of legacy is a very important one to address.

At the very beginning I told you that the meaning of life is the pursuit of happiness, and that is truly what I believe, from the depths of my heart, but some people might want more, might ask for more of a direction, and it could argued that this is a valid other option for the question of "what is the meaning of life?" Because legacy, legacy is something that plays on all our minds at some point.

It is the one other thing we never need to be told isn't it? You're born, you grow, and from such a young age you start to think,

"What do I want to be when I grow up?" "What do I want to do with my life?" When you get a little older it becomes "how will I be remembered?" Because at some point that becomes what we want, we are all terrified of death on some level, so we seek to leave something behind, because that way we are never really one hundred percent gone are we?

so we leave behind kids, ideas, memories and a multitude of other things, its why the world has embraced such a celebrity fuelled culture in recent years, well I say recent years we have been doing in for thousands of them, from Tutankhamen all the way up to Elvis, Kim Kardasian and Justin Bieber and regardless of your feelings toward any of them, them will be remembered along time after we are gone.

legacy, the corner-stone of human civilisation, mankind built pyramids, sailed the seas, filled in the blank corners of the map, we as a species have split the atom, and explored the cold oblivion of space, we have no wings yet we fly the skies the world over.

millions of men and women of the human race have made themselves immortal through their accomplishments, but we all leave something behind,

regardless of who we are, be it a thought, an idea, a memory or even just a smile at the thought of us on someone we love's lips.
And not to sound sappy, but can't that be enough?

For most of us that might be all there is, or once was, but now days social media being what it is, there is more and more of a record of whowe were after we are gone, you don't need to be rich or famous for your descendants to be able to know everything about you now. Funny thought isn't it? That your great great grandchild might end up looking you up on Facebook for history homework?

Rule 19 Summary

<u>Leave something worth remembering.</u>

Rule 20: Offence

This one's kind of a negative chapter, because I'm going to be chastising a large amount of the readers, but even so it's something that does need to be said. Listen its fine to take offence to something that is genuinely offensive, and I understand that what any of us find offensive is a matter of opinion, and not a universal thing, but even so, some people need to catch themselves the fuck on.

There are people out there who will take great personal offence with literally everything and anything, hell its gotten so bad that some people can make a whole career out of offending others, where as even ten, twenty years ago, no one would have paid them any mind, where as now days they can cash checks with the attention they get, ok listen this current global level of like hyper vigilance against anything controversial probably does come from a good place, people are trying to stamp out intolerance and what not, but it's gotten seriously out of hand, and worse its having the negative effect on the argument sometimes.

It's ok to be offended by something offensive, by something you don't see as right, by something that's wrong, trying to pass itself off as something that's ok, but not everything is like that, this world can be a beautiful place, if you let it be, if you just drown out the trolls and the jackasses, don't give them the time of day, I can't stress enough how much people are manipulated by offence.

Let us say I can offend you, really get your goat up, then by getting you to express your offence at me, I've manipulated you into spreading awareness of me, and in an age where everybody has a voice, and it's easier than ever to express your opinion, I've used you without your knowledge to push myself to a larger audience, and this is exactly what some people do.

So don't give those people power through you, even with the best intentions, even by condemning their actions. You are just adding fuel to the fire, and making their voice louder, really what I'm trying to say is, if you find something offensive to you, stop and think about it, think about why it offends you, and think about why it was created, or shared or thought up, and if it was created for the sole purpose of offending people like you, then straight up ignore it, in fact boycott it if possible, that's how you rob people of doing this or their power. Cause all they want is your attention, be it positive or negative, it makes no difference to them.

Rule 20: Summary

<u>Ask yourself why?</u>

Rule 21: Ego

Ego is important and more good than bad honestly, people with large egos might come across as jackasses on occasion, but what do they care? They don't, their ego won't allow it. People with big egos are also generally more successful, maybe because there are a lot of similarities between ego and confidence. They generally bounce back from setbacks quicker too.

Ego is usually one of the best defences against negativity, and when it comes to you or I, it's hard, maybe impossible to pin point where opinion stops and ego starts, I think I'm a good writer, I mean I'm wrote a book after all, but is that my ego telling me that, or a genuine reflection of skill? I can't tell, you can in my case, but I cannot for myself.

The only real downside to a big ego as I said before is that occasionally you'll come across as a bit of a jackass, and the bigger the ego the more jackassery involved, but that really only applies to truck sized egos, on the other hand though, if you can back it up, not a jackass.

So take stock of yourself, take your positives and your skills and the best of yourself, and celebrate it, the more positivity you can have in your life, the better it gets.

That said, don't embellish the things you can't do, or the qualities you don't have, that's not ego, that's just lying to yourself, and the complete opposite of everything I'm trying to tell you with this book. It's very hard to decide what's ego and what's confidence, the two may as well be one and the same most of the time, so fake it till you make it as they say, and think on this in the future, because just maybe, it'll will make you stronger.

I've touched on the negatives of this already and as with anything, excess is kind of what leads to ruin but there is another negative side that I have not mentioned. Meekness, and I don't mean to butt heads with anyone's religion, but personally that whole "The meek will inherit the earth" thing?
Sounds like a con to me, like a real

"Don't worry if we are kicking the shit out of you now, one day all this will be yours (when we are done with it)" Kind of deal. Listen as I said I'm not trying to butt heads with anyone over their religion, just because I don't share someone's faith, doesn't mean I will judge them negatively for having it, if you are of a religious disposition and you take offence at my previous comment, just Know, I am from northern Ireland, we kind of have a monopoly on religious offence by this point.

Rule 21 Summary

Rule 22: Outlook

I don't want to get bogged down with the negatives in life, something that can be far too easy to do now days, although maybe it's always been like that?

Life is great and it is terrible, we struggle and succeed, sometimes we fail but that doesn't give us any right or reason to stop. Cause maybe, just maybe it is the struggle that makes it all real?
It is in the struggle of it all that we earn our real strength, or we find the strength that has been there the whole time?

You are you, and you are unique, believe it or not? You have no idea how special you really are, but let me tell you just one thing that you don't realise about yourself, regardless of what you believe religiously, spiritually, emotionally let me remind you of the astounding series of events that put you right here, right now reading these words.

Once, your ancestors found each other, found love or solace or whatever else they sought in each other and conceived a child, that child was an ancestor to you. That is a cycle that goes back all the way to the beginning, and all the way down. Through time, through all of human history to you, so that you could be born, so that you could live the life you live, experience all that you have experienced, and be who you are, You at one point will be, or once were the last link in that chain, and if you should have children then you are passing that along, that responsibility, that legacy, that awesome fact. That in some way, all of human history has culminated in you.

But still, that's only how I see you, and I'm nothing to you, so imagine how you must appear to other people? A lot of life is in how you see it, and I can't tell you what your outlook should be, I don't have the right nor do I have the reason, I could bullshit you, don't get me wrong, I could tell you to "find the light inside" or "embrace each day as a victory" and a million other things, but what would be the point? Your outlook is up you, take what you want from the world, and how you choose to see it, personally I am a horrible cynic, but also an optimist, and an old romantic at heart, now that's a confusing outlook.

But I'm still the same as you, most of the time I have no idea what I'm doing, and just hoping it ends well. So as a personal favour to me, think about how you see the world, and if you're happy with how it seems to you, great, but if not, take steps to change it.

How we see the world in a large way impacts how this world is, and for all its faults, and mistakes and beauty and horror, and everything it is, I still love this world.

Rule 22 Summary

<u>Everything is in the eye of the beholder.</u>

Rule 23: Dedication

Dedication towards what we want is an essential part of finding happiness, because everyone knows that anything worth having doesn't come easy, and when you struggle, you work and finally you triumph, it's so much more worth it isn't it?

I can't stress how important dedication is, and you know I'm right, every factor in your life is directly linked to how dedicated you are to it, from your career, to your relationships, even your hobbies and interests it all ties together.

I'm lazy in some respects I can admit that, mostly cause its true, but I'm not an idiot so I'm never lazy when it counts. When you benefit from effort why not put in that effort? And I know that's there's a lot of things you can just kind of skate by on, in the past I've been more than happy to do so in regards to a lot of things, and although I'm still quite young as I got older I realised the folly in that. Truly I'm thankful that I realised that at any age, even better at this age, but that's the same for all of us whether you are eight or eighty, you've still got a life to live.

I find it weird that today's culture kind of frowns on trying, like its mocked by people with a "too cool for school" mentality, where I grew up you were weird if you read books, and it's the strangest thing, we as a culture worldwide for some unknown reason over the past few generations decided to mock intelligence, or precedence. There is a term "Try hard" for people who try too hard, seriously what the fuck happened to us? We are the species which without fins worked out how to traverse thousands of miles of water, which without wings worked out how to fly, we put a human being on the damn moon, and we have minds that as we speak are cracking the secrets of the universe wide open.

You think any of that came easy? You think any of that didn't take perseverance and unfathomable dedication? So what's your excuse for not trying? What's anyone's?

I'm not saying you have to have a serious personality or anything, or you can't have fun, or that your every second must be spent working toward some goal, I know it sounded like I was, just don't half ass things, it's not that hard, you know what you want out of life, so put the effort in for it.

Rule 23 Summary

Effort is no excuse.

Rule 24: Dreams & Aspirations

All of us have dreams and aspirations, things we want to do in this life, and a lot of us give up on those things, maybe life gets in the way, or we find something better, or we find out that it's not really what we expected, still whatever the reason, and some of them are good and valid, it still stings a little doesn't it? But that's life; we don't get to do everything we wanted and that's sad, but ask yourself, what's stopping you? What is stopping you from following your dreams?

If they are still important to you, what's your reason for not pursuing them?

Remember when you were a child? Life was much simpler; most of us knew what we wanted to be when we were grown, I say most of us, because I had no idea, still don't really. But as I got older, I always wanted to write, and this is me pursuing that dream now, and it might not be much in the grand scheme of things, or even in the grand scheme of my life, but it feels great, it feels great to do this, and to know that you are reading my words, that maybe you feel some connection to me, or to my view of the world, but think back on a younger you, how you felt and how you thought, and ask yourself what would they want you to be doing with your life?

I know that sounds blunt, and extreme, but I am trying to motivate you, maybe poorly but still, I hope you get my point, take the things that used to be important to you, take the things that still are and find what you want to be doing, what you want to be, I don't know you, I don't know your situation, but I know your capable of anything if you put your mind to it, because I am, and everyone else is, so so are you. And to anyone who did grow up to follow their dreams, to all the firemen, and astronauts, and celebrities who may well be reading this, kudos, you rock, good work.

But the majority of people are not like you lot, the majority of us, really have no idea what we are doing, we know what we should be doing, but that's hard, and a lot of us are quite lazy, and we know in our heart of hearts that there is no one, nor nothing to blame but ourselves.

But still maybe a little reminder can go a long way, and you reading this now, maybe you're not living up to what you wanted to do, or be, and maybe your reason for not doing that isn't good enough to you, in which case.

Hop to it, you only get one go round (except the Buddhists, if those dudes are right) so why wouldn't you make it count? Good luck, I'm rooting for you.

Rule 24: Summary

<u>What did you want to be when you grew up?</u>

Rule 25: Happiness and its pursuit

I told you at the beginning the meaning of life, and can you really argue against it? And even if you can, can you say I am wrong, don't you value your own happiness? Don't your actions toward others bring you some measure of it? I've said so much in this book, and yet it feels like I have said nothing at all, because your happiness isn't up to me to give to you, it's up to you to find, to pursue it.

your happiness is yours to find, because this life is your path to walk, and whatever gives you the strength to walk it, to run or sprint it, that is your strength, that is who you really are, and if ever you feel tired, if ever you feel weak or like you cannot go on, then search for that strength, in yourself or in others, because you will always find it, because it is always there, it might take a while to find it sometimes but if you keep looking, keep moving forward, keep up your pursuit, and you will find that your happiness is well within reach.

I can only hope that I am wrong that I have said nothing at all to you, because these words you've been reading, this entire book, it's never intended to tell you what to do, to coddle you or to pander to you. This book is my thoughts on life, on happiness and on you.

Whoever you are, out there in the world, your hopes and dreams, your fears and your fantasies I wish you nothing but luck, in your pursuit of happiness.

So take what you will from this book, it's my gift to you, if I have said anything that will stick with you, anything that will be of use in your life from now on. Thank you because I have taken some measure of happiness in writing it, and feel nothing but pride that my words might have touched you, might in some small way inhabit who you are and who you will become.

Table of summaries

Rule 1: Forgiveness: Life is too short for the baggage.

Rule 2: Choice and consequence: Think before you act.

Rule 3: Opinion: We don't all get to have an opinion.

Rule 4: The importance of words: You can't unsay things so say what sticks.

Rule 5: Sorry: Sorry when sorry is due.

Rule 6: Acceptance & death: When life gives you lemons.

Rule 7: Love: Love is love need I say more?

Rule 8: Excess: If some is good, more must be better: Sometimes just enough, is all you need.

Rule 9: Patience: Early birds, worms and such.

Rule 10: Change: Change is changing.

Rule 11: Anxiety: Push down the wall.

Rule 12: Depression: Give it time.

Rule 13: Importance of fun: Life is short; don't let it be short and boring.

Rule 14: Action & Duality of human nature: You are more than one thing.

Rule 15: Anger: Anger is the dog in all of us, but it is our choice if it barks, or it bites.

Rule 16: Courage: One spark can light a fuse, because sometimes one spark is all it takes.

Rule 17: Honesty: You know not to trust dishonest people, so why be dishonest?

Rule 18: Connections: Who would you bleed for?Life is too short for matching socks.

Rule 19: Legacy: Leave something worth remembering.

Rule 20: Offence: Ask yourself why?

Rule 21: Ego: Beware Jackassery.

Rule 22: Outlook: **Everything is in the eye of the beholder.**

Rule 23: Dedication: **Effort is no excuse.**

Rule 24: Dreams & Aspirations: **What did you want to be when you grew up?**

Rule 25: Happiness and its pursuit: **Pursue your own happiness.**

www.ingramcontent.com/pod-product-compliance
Lightning Source LLC
Chambersburg PA
CBHW031810150726
47989CB00006B/2945